Sports Illustrated KIDS

BASEBALL'S BIGGEST RIVALRIES

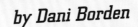

by Dani Borden

CAPSTONE PRESS
a capstone imprint

Published by Capstone Press, an imprint of Capstone
1710 Roe Crest Drive, North Mankato, Minnesota 56003
capstonepub.com

SPORTS ILLUSTRATED KIDS is a trademark of ABG-SI LLC. Used with permission.

Library of Congress Cataloging-in-Publication Data
Names: Nash, Sibylla, author.
Title: Baseball's biggest rivalries / by Sibylla Nash.
Description: North Mankato, Minnesota : Capstone Press, [2024] | Series: Sports illustrated kids. Great sports rivalries | Includes bibliographical references and index. | Audience: Ages 8 to 11 | Audience: Grades 4-6 | Summary: "What makes a good rivalry? Sometimes it's two teams going head-to-head. Sometimes it's two players trying to one-up each other. Sometimes it's fans egging each other on. Baseball is full of rivalries just like these. From college clashes to major league matchups, read on to discover some of the sports' biggest rivalries."—Provided by publisher.
Identifiers: LCCN 2022047829 (print) | LCCN 2022047830 (ebook) | ISBN 9781669048961 (hardcover) | ISBN 9781669048916 (paperback) | ISBN 9781669048923 (pdf) | ISBN 9781669048947 (kindle edition) | ISBN 9781669048954 (epub)
Subjects: LCSH: Baseball–United States—History—Juvenile literature. | Sports rivalries—United States—History—Juvenile literature.
Classification: LCC GV863.A1 N366 2024 (print) | LCC GV863.A1 (ebook) | DDC 796.357/64—dc23/eng/20221013
LC record available at https://lccn.loc.gov/2022047829
LC ebook record available at https://lccn.loc.gov/2022047830

Editorial Credits
Editor: Alison Deering; Designer: Elyse White; Media Researcher: Rebekah Hubstenberger; Production Specialist: Whitney Schaefer

Image Credits and Design Elements
Dreamstime: Jerry Coli, 15; Getty Images: Bettmann, 6, 8, C. Morgan Engel/NCAA Photos, 11, Daniel Shirey/MLB Photos, 4, David J. Griffin/Icon Sportswire, 21, Jamie Squire/Allsport, 14, Jason O. Watson, 5, Jim Davis/The Boston Globe, 7, Jim McIsaac, 27, MLB Photos, 25, Olen Collection/Diamond Images, 29, Stephen Dunn, 24; Library of Congress, 12 (all); Shutterstock: Danler, 10, Jansx Customs, design element (lines), luma_art, 20, Shiboshi, design element (baseball icon), vectortatu, design element (vs.); Sports Illustrated: Chuck Solomon, cover (top left), Damian Strohmeyer, cover (top right), Heinz Kluetmeier, 17, Robert Beck, 23, SI Cover/John Iacono, 28, SI Cover/John W. McDonough, 18

TABLE OF CONTENTS

Words in **bold** are in the glossary.

Batter Up!

What makes a good rivalry? Sometimes it's two teams going head-to-head. Sometimes it's two players trying to one-up each other. Sometimes it's fans egging each other on.

Baseball is full of rivalries just like these. From college clashes to major league matchups, read on to discover some of the sports' biggest rivalries.

Rivalries between teams can lead to fierce competition during games.

Arguments sometimes erupt between rival players on the field.

Chapter 1

Back-in-the-Day Rivals

Some rivalries have long histories. In fact, many are as old as the sport itself.

Boston Red Sox vs. New York Yankees

The rivalry between the Red Sox and the Yankees is one of the longest in Major League Baseball (MLB). It goes back more than a **century**.

The Red Sox won five championships between 1903 and 1918. They were the best team in the league. But in 1919, the Sox owner kickstarted a **fierce** rivalry. He sold the team's star player, Babe Ruth, to the Yankees. It is thought to be the worst trade in baseball history.

The 1921 New York Yankees with Babe Ruth (middle row, fourth from the right)

Tensions boiled over between Yankees and Red Sox players during a 2018 game at Fenway Park in Boston, Massachusetts.

The Yankees went on to win four World Series with Ruth. Meanwhile the Sox went 86 years without winning a World Series. After 1918, they didn't win again until 2004!

Stats

Total matchups	Most wins
2,320	Yankees (1,257)
Biggest wins	
Yankees: 22–1 (2000)	Red Sox: 19–3 (2019)
World Series titles	
Yankees: 27	Red Sox: 9

Los Angeles Dodgers vs. San Francisco Giants

These West Coast teams started out as neighbors in New York. The Giants formed in Manhattan in 1883. The Dodgers took the field in Brooklyn in 1890. They have been rivals ever since.

In 1957, both teams moved to California. They took their rivalry with them. The Giants beat the Dodgers twice in tiebreaker games to win the **National League** (NL) **pennant**.

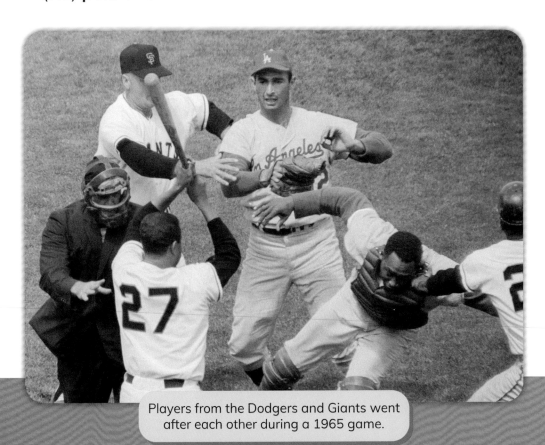

Players from the Dodgers and Giants went after each other during a 1965 game.

The wins only increased the tension. In 1965, the Giants pitcher hit the Dodgers catcher in the head with a bat. He needed 14 stitches.

These two teams have been evenly matched for 133 seasons. They both hold more pennants than any other NL team.

Stats

Total matchups	Most wins
2,559	Giants (1,274)
Biggest wins	
Giants: 26–8 (1944)	Dodgers: 17–0 (2014)
World Series titles	
Giants: 8	Dodgers: 7
National League pennants	
Giants: 23	Dodgers: 24

Fun Fact

In 2005, the Giants became the first pro sports team to win 10,000 games. They did so by beating the Dodgers 4–3.

Mississippi State vs. University of Mississippi

The rivalry between the Mississippi State Bulldogs and the University of Mississippi (Ole Miss) Rebels is more than 100 years old. This competition is based on location. The schools are less than 100 miles (161 kilometers) from each other.

The two teams face off in the Governor's Cup. The game has been around since 1980. It used to be called the Mayor's Trophy. Mississippi has won 22 times. Ole Miss has won 19 times.

In 2021, the Bulldogs won the National Collegiate Athletic Association (NCAA) Division I championship. The Rebels took the title in 2022. These back-to-back wins gave fans across Mississippi bragging rights in college baseball.

The Ole Miss Rebels celebrated after winning the 2022 Division I Men's Baseball Championship.

Stats

Total matchups	Most wins
472	Mississippi State (259)
College World Series wins	
Ole Miss: 1	Mississippi: 1
NCAA Regional Championship wins	
Ole Miss: 12	Mississippi: 16
SEC Tournament wins	
Ole Miss: 3	Mississippi: 7

Chapter 2

Frenemies

Some rivalries start with friendly competition between players from different teams. But rivalries are even more interesting if the players are teammates!

Babe Ruth vs. Ty Cobb

In the early 1900s, Babe Ruth and Ty Cobb were two of baseball's biggest superstars. Ruth was a pitcher and powerful hitter known for his home runs. Outfielder Cobb was famous for his base running and ability to hit to all fields.

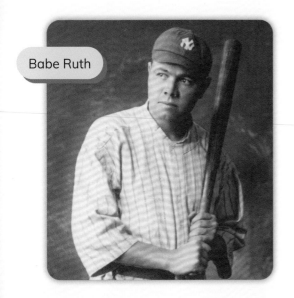

Babe Ruth

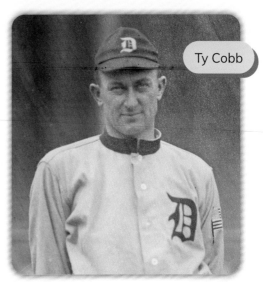

Ty Cobb

For years, the two competed to be the best. In June 1921, Ruth and the New York Yankees went head-to-head with Cobb and the Detroit Tigers. The Yankees swept the Tigers in the four-game series.

The rivalry extended off the field as well. Ruth was asked to take a photo with Cobb during the series. He refused.

Ruth and Cobb are still considered two of the greatest to ever play the sport. Both men were inducted into the Baseball Hall of Fame in 1936.

Career Stats

	Babe Ruth	Ty Cobb
Games played	2,503	3,034
At-bats	8,399	11,440
Runs	2,174	2,245
Home runs	714	117
Stolen bases	123	897

Derek Jeter vs. Alex Rodriguez

Derek Jeter and Alex "A-Rod" Rodriguez started out as best buds. The two shortstops met in 1993 at a college game. They were BFFs through their time in the minor leagues and into the majors.

A-Rod (left) and Jeter (right) share a laugh on the field.

The friendship between the two star players took a turn after A-Rod signed with the Rangers.

Things changed in 2000. Rodriguez signed a 10-year deal with the Texas Rangers. It was worth $252 million. At the time, it was the largest deal in baseball history. Soon after, A-Rod did an interview with ESPN. He said Jeter wouldn't be able to beat his contract.

The next year, the New York Yankees signed a $189 million deal with Jeter. A-Rod gave another interview. He said that Jeter, ". . . never had to lead. He can just go and play and have fun."

In 2004, A-Rod was traded to the Yankees. He moved to third base. Jeter stayed at shortstop. The two were teammates for 10 years. They won one World Series together in 2009 and **retired** within two years of one another. Jeter retired in 2014. Rodriguez followed in 2016.

Years later, their rivalry still stands. In 2022, Jeter said that Rodriguez was "not a true friend." Fans are split on who's the best. Both have impressive stats. So far, only Jeter is in the Baseball Hall of Fame.

Career Stats

	Derek Jeter	Alex Rodriguez
Games played	2,747	2,784
Hits	3,465	3,115
At-bats	11,195	10,566
Runs	1,923	2,021
Home runs	260	696
Stolen bases	358	329
World Series wins	5	1

Jeter (left) and A-Rod (right) stand together in the Yankees dugout.

Chapter 3

Crosstown Competition

Competition can be even more intense when two teams are in the same city. These rivalries can leave fans divided.

Chicago Cubs vs. Chicago White Sox

The rivalry between the Cubs and the White Sox dates all the way back to 1906. That's when the teams faced off in the World Series. The meetup marked the first time two teams from the same city had ever competed in a World Series.

A 2020 magazine cover highlighted the rivalry.

The White Sox went into the series with the worst batting average in the **American League** (AL). They were called the Hitless Wonders. The Cubs had won a record-breaking 116 games. Despite that, the Sox made history. They won the series four games to two.

Today, Chicago is split. The Cubs play on the North Side. The Sox have the South Side. It's an ongoing battle between two teams determined to be Chicago's best.

Stats

Total matchups	Most wins
144	White Sox (77, including 73 regular season wins)
Biggest wins	
White Sox: 13–1 (2021)	Cubs: 10–0 (2020)
World Series wins	
White Sox: 3	Cubs: 3

Fun Fact

The Cubs hold the record for longest World Series drought in MLB history. They went 107 seasons without winning between 1909 and 2016. The White Sox are right behind them with an 87-year drought.

Georgia Tech vs. University of Georgia (UGA)

Only 70 miles (113 km) separate the Georgia Bulldogs from the Georgia Tech Yellow Jackets. The colleges have been competitors since the 1890s. But the one thing they can agree on is their rivalry. It's a "Clean, Old-Fashioned Hate" between the two schools.

This rivalry is big city vs. small college town, and fans are passionate. So far only UGA has won a national title. But it's not just bragging rights at stake. These two schools also compete for funding and potential students.

Georgia

UGA

Georgia Tech

Every year the teams put their rivalry to good use. They play for charity in the Spring Classic for Kids.

Fun Fact

The 2004 Georgia vs. Georgia Tech game at Turner Field had the second most spectators in college baseball history. 28,836 visitors turned out to watch the Bulldogs win.

Georgia Tech's Drew Compton (right) held UGA's Cole Tate (left) on base during a 2020 game.

Stats

Total matchups	Most wins
350	UGA (199)

NCAA Tournament matchups	Most wins
6	UGA (4)

Chapter 4

Most Competitive Teams

Competition is fierce in the major leagues. But some teams are in a league of their own when it comes to rivalries.

Houston Astros

The Astros played in the National League for 51 seasons. In 2013, they moved to the American League. They're the first team to make the World Series in each league. And they've picked up plenty of rivals along the way.

Astros vs. Los Angeles Dodgers

The Astros played the Dodgers at least 18 times a season in the National League. Their rivalry has been filled with division title tie breakers and Most Valuable Player (MVP) arguments.

Their 2017 World Series matchup also included cheating claims. The Astros ultimately won four games to three. It was their first World Series win.

Astros players celebrated after defeating the Dodgers in the 2017 World Series.

Key Matchups

NL West tie breaker (October 6, 1980)
The Astros defeat the Dodgers 7–1 and head into the postseason for the first time.

NL Division title (October 11, 1981)
The Dodgers shut out the Astros 4–0 in the final game of the series. They won the series three games to two and went on to win the World Series.

Astros vs. St. Louis Cardinals

This was one of the best NL rivalries in the early 2000s. From 1996 to 2002 and 2004 to 2006, either the Astros or the Cardinals won the NL Central Division. Six of those wins belonged to the Cardinals. Four belonged to the Astros.

The two teams also faced off in 2004 and 2005 in the NL Championship series. The first year, the Cardinals won the series four games to three. The next year, it was the Astros. They won the series four games to two.

Fans on both sides are passionate about the rivalry between the two teams.

Key Matchups

NL Championship (October 21, 2004)
The Cardinals win game seven 5–2. (They win the series four games to three.) The Astros lose their chance to play in their first World Series.

NL Championship (October 19, 2005)
The Astros defeat the Cardinals four games to two. They advance to the World Series for the first time in their history.

Astros vs. Atlanta Braves

These two teams battled it out for 25 years in the NL West Division. Then they moved to different divisions and became playoff rivals. In the 1990s, the Braves owned this rivalry. They knocked the Astros out of the playoffs three times in five years.

It was a different story in 2004 and 2005. The Astros beat the Braves, including an 18-inning game four in 2005.

The teams also went head-to-head in the 2021 World Series. The Braves beat the Astros in six games.

Braves players celebrated after winning Game 6 of the World Series against the Astros in 2021.

Key Matchups

NL Division series (October 12, 2001)
The Braves win Game 3 by a score of 6-2, and **sweep** the series over the Astros.

NL Division series (October 9, 2005)
The Astros score a home run in the 18th inning and defeat the Braves three games to two. At the time, this was the longest postseason game in baseball history.

New York Yankees

Sometimes it seems like it's the Yankees (AL) against the world. The team has been around since 1901. Their long history makes it easy to rack up rivalries.

Yankees vs. Los Angeles Dodgers

This rivalry is one of baseball's most famous. The Yankees and the Dodgers (NL) first squared off in the 1941 World Series. The Yankees won in five games. They beat the Dodgers again in 1947, 1949, 1952, and 1953. The Dodgers beat the Yankees in the 1955 Series. But the Yankees came back to win in 1956.

Stats

World Series wins	
Yankees	27 total, 8 against the Dodgers
Dodgers	7 total, 3 against the Yankees

Famous Yankees

Yogi Berra, Joe DiMaggio, Derek Jeter, Lou Gehrig, Mikey Mantle, Babe Ruth

Famous Dodgers

Roy Campanella, Clayton Kershaw, Sandy Koufax, Mike Piazza, Jackie Robinson

In total, the two teams have faced off in 11 World Series. That's more than any other pair of teams in the American and National Leagues. They haven't met in a World Series since 1981, but the rivalry is still ongoing.

Players give their all, especially during rivalry games.

Yankees vs. New York Mets

The Yankees and the Mets (NL) battle it out in the **interleague** Subway Series. The Yankees won the first matchup in 1997. Things got heated in 2000. Yankees pitcher Roger Clemens hit Mets catcher Mike Piazza in the helmet with a fastball.

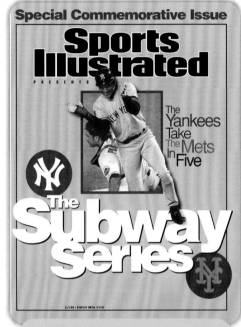

A magazine cover celebrates the Yankees Subway Series win.

Tensions were high when the teams met in the World Series that year. In Game 2, Piazza hit a pitch from Clemens so hard his bat shattered Clemens threw a piece of the bat to first base. It almost hit Piazza. Both teams stormed the field. The Yankees still won the series four games to one.

Stats

Total matchups	Most wins
138	Yankees (82)

Key Matchup

2000 World Series—Yankees win four games to one

Yankees vs. San Francisco Giants

The Yankees and Giants (NL) used to share the same stadium! When the Giants were in New York, they owned the ballpark where the Yankees played. The Giants' owner wanted to kick out the Yankees. Babe Ruth and the rest of the team were too popular!

In 1962, the teams met in the World Series. It was their first matchup since the Giants left New York. The Giants were favored to win. Instead, the Yankees won four games to three.

The 1962 World Series marked a major matchup between the rival teams.

Because they're in different leagues, the Yankees and Giants usually only compete during the World Series. Fans can watch them compete during the regular season in interleague play.

Stats

World Series matchups—7 (Yankees: 5, Giants: 2)

Glossary

American League (uh-MER-i-kuhn LEEG)—one of two major leagues in professional U.S. baseball; both leagues have 15 teams

century (SEN-chuh-ree)—a period of 100 years

fierce (FEERSS)—characterized by extreme force, intensity, or anger

interleague (in-tur-LEEG)—regular-season games played between an American League and National League team in Major League Baseball

National League (NASH-uh-nuhl LEEG)—one of two major leagues in professional U.S. baseball; both leagues have 15 teams and each league is divided into three geographic divisions: East, Central, and West

pennant (PEN-uhnt)—a triangular flag that symbolizes a league championship

retire (ri-TIRE)—to give up work usually because of a person's age

sweep (SWEEP)—when a team wins all the games in a series without losing to the opposing team

Read More

Berglund, Bruce. *Baseball GOATs: The Greatest Athletes of All Time*. North Mankato, MN: Capstone, 2022.

Coleman, Ted. *Boston Red Sox: All-Time Greats*. Mendota Heights, MN: North Star Editions, 2022.

Jacobs, Greg. *The Everything Kids' Baseball Book*. Avon, MS: Adams Media, 2020.

Internet Sites

MLB Kids
mlb.com/fans/kids

National Baseball Hall of Fame
baseballhall.org

Sports Illustrated Kids: Baseball
sikids.com/baseball

Index

About the Author

Dani Borden is a writer based in Los Angeles, California. She enjoys learning and researching new topics to write about. Previously a dog-person, she now has two cats and has been known to root for the Atlanta Braves.

photo credit: Leah Ford